RISE FROM THE SHADOWS

OVERCOME YOUR PAST, RECLAIM YOUR VOICE, LIVE YOUR LIGHT

EMEM WASHINGTON

Rise From The Shadows: Overcome Your Past,
Reclaim Your Voice, Live Your Light

Published by Emem Washington Publishing, Houston TX USA

Published in the United States of America

Editor: Chris O'Byrne
Author's Photo: Inez Lara
Front Cover Design: German Creative

Scripture unless otherwise indicated taken from the Holy Bible, the King James Version. Public domain.

Paperback ISBN-13: 978-0-578-47623-0

Also available in E-book format

DEDICATION

This book is dedicated to my beloved mother, the late Mrs. Nene Akpaffiong, for believing in this big dreamer from day one. Your belief in "me and my dreams" still pushes me to this day. I love and miss you, Mommy.

This book is also dedicated to my family. Thank you for your prayers and the lifetime of encouragement you have given me. Thank you, Dad, for instilling the value of education, hard work, and reading in us.

Last, but most importantly, this book is dedicated to my heavenly Father, who has truly been my Rock and the ultimate Cheerleader. Thank You, Lord, for making all things beautiful in Your own time.

CONTENTS

ACKNOWLEDGMENTS

There are several people who contributed in some way to making it possible for this book to happen.

My sincere thanks Shaneequa Cannon for accepting me into her inaugural Walking in AUTHORity course, which provided the foundational information I needed to start writing this book, and the encouragement that what I had to say was needed.

A huge thank you also to Chris O'Byrne for editing this book and helping me get my message out effectively.

Thank you also to Jokotade for your suggestions on the title. Shout out to of my "Thrive Beyond" Facebook community members for helping me decide on this book cover. And a special thank you to my social media family at-large (on all the various platforms) who continue to show love. It means more than I can say. Thank you.

INTRODUCTION

We are all meant to shine, as children do. We were born to make manifest the glory of God within us. It is not just in some; it is in everyone.

- Marianne Williamson

They are all around you. You see them every day. Or maybe you see right over them. They are in plain sight, and yet they are hidden. You pass them in hallways, you sit next to them in church, and you listen to their presentations in meetings at work. Regular people just like you and me, who are in plain sight, and yet they are hiding. We hear them talk, we see them laugh, but it is not their authentic selves we see and hear. They have put on masks and are hiding their true selves.

Some hide because of how others have treated them. Others hide because they are introverts or they are shy. And then there are those who are hidden because their past, their stories, have caused them to build a thick wall around them, blocking them from being seen.

Sadly, some of the most brilliant minds, the most talented treasures, the most exquisite gems, remain hidden. I call them hidden gems. They have so much to offer, and yet they remain buried in dust, hidden in the shadows, and many never make a reappearance, and their brightness is never reignited.

This is not God's plan for them. This is not God's plan for you. Consider this your wakeup call to come out of hiding, show up as your authentic self, and stop merely displaying a shadow of who you truly are. Come out of the shadows and shine your light. You are a light. God has given you a light that you are to share with the world.

Now, don't get nervous when I say that you are to share your light with the world because I don't necessarily mean out in front of cameras for the whole world to see. The world for you might mean your family, your home, your job, your church, or it might literally mean the world. The point is, you cannot keep your light buried any longer.

In Matthew Chapter 5, Jesus says, "Ye are the light of the world. A city that is set on a hill cannot be hid. Neither do men light a candle and put it under a bushel, but on a candlestick; and it giveth light unto all that are in the house. Let your light so shine before men, that they may see your good works, and glorify your Father which is in heaven."

You are a light. The real you may not be perfect, but the real you is a light that does not need to be kept hidden. I didn't say it, Jesus did.

While this book is not an autobiography, I do share a piece of my story. The easiest way for me to illustrate how to rise from the shadows is to share a bit of my journey. As you read the words on the pages that follow, my hope is that what I share will serve as your passport to lasting transformation from a life in the shadows to a life where you allow your true light to shine as the uniquely crafted person God has created you to be. Are you ready? Let's go!

1

MY SHADOW STORY

There is no greater agony than bearing an untold story inside you.

- Maya Angelou

My sons often ask me what superpowers I possess. I usually struggle to come up with a response, but in recent years, I have come to realize that I have always been an advocate for others, especially the overlooked and excluded. You will typically find me rooting for the underdog. Advocacy is not an exciting superpower to my preteen sons, but I believe advocacy *is* one of my superpowers. And as a life coach for women, I have the privilege of advocating for my clients by guiding them through facing fears, elevating their self-worth, and encouraging them to show up as victors and not victims. The fact that I have had to do all of this in my own life helps me better serve my clients as I guide them through their own journeys.

My sons would probably be far more interested in my response if I told them that my superpower was the ability to mimic anyone else or the ability to become invisible at will. Those are wonderful superpowers in movies, but in everyday life, they do not always serve us well. I know because I spent many years operating in the realm of mimicry and invisibility. I hid my authentic self by either mimicking other people or by revealing a false version of myself. I know now that I was not the only one, that there are many all over the world who sadly feel the need to hide.

Thankfully, over time, I finally realized the importance of showing up as my authentic self, quirks and all. As a result, I no longer live in a constant state of unhappiness, being envious of others who are living up to their full potentials while my life passes me by. My relationships are richer, my life is fuller, and my children are empowered to find and use their own voices.

"Hey," the boy called out to me as I walked down the hall to my next class. "He like' you," he said, pointing to one of the other boys standing in the mini huddle. Holding back tears, I rushed on to my next class, trying to shut out their mocking laughter. I wasn't being rude by ignoring him; on the contrary, he and his friends thought it was fun to target girls they thought were ugly and say that one of them liked her. Then, they'd laugh loudly and cause a ruckus, drawing more attention to the girl from other passers-by.

As far as I could recall, I had cried more times since starting at this new school, than I had in my entire life. We had just moved back to the U.S. after my family moved away when I was 4. I was 12 years old, and my family had just moved from Nigeria back to Houston. I had lived in 3 countries on 3 continents by this time, and making friends had never been a problem. How do you go from being one of the most popular kids in your school or at least one of the most liked to being made fun of every day several times a day?

I didn't know it at the time, but that year, my 8th-grade year would be one of the most pivotal years of my life. It would be the year that I sought out all the different ways to become invisible, ways to make myself blend in and not stand out.

Why couldn't the kids treat me like they treated each other instead of calling me mean names like "African booty scratcher" or asking me if I missed swinging on trees with monkeys? And just when I thought I had "fixed" one thing about myself, they would find something else about me to make fun of.

That school year had actually started out as an exciting year for me. I had begun the school year in Calabar, a city in southern Nigeria. My parents had called us downstairs one day to tell us that we were moving back to the U.S., but we were not to tell our classmates, our friends, or anyone else. Our parents would be the ones to tell those who needed to know. I obliged for as long as I could, but how could I keep this from my best friends? Surely they needed to know this exciting news and what it meant, not just for me, but for them! So I told my inner circle and made them promise not to tell anyone else. My imagination ran wild at everything I would experience when we moved back to America. Moving to America meant lots of chocolates and dolls, and I promised my friends that I would send them both. We would probably live in a high rise like they did on *Diff'rent Strokes*. Or maybe we would live on a fun street like the one on *Sesame Street*. Oh yes, this school year was shaping out to be my most exciting year yet.

And yet it very quickly became my most difficult year to date. I arrived in the U.S. a bony 12-year-old, but within 6 months my skinny body began to take on a life of its own as puberty took over. My face began to stay greasy all day, and pimples popped out anywhere they could find space on my face. I literally thought I had an incurable disease the day I noticed stretch marks on my thighs until my mom explained what those were. I had gained so much weight so quickly trying out all the different cuisines America had to offer, from pizza to hamburgers and fries to milkshakes and all other kinds of junk food.

And so it was during this exciting but awkward time in my life that I found myself in 8th grade in a school with many people that looked like me, but try as I did, I could not fit in. I would cry at home almost every day, but my mom didn't seem to understand my plight. Of course she didn't; she was gorgeous and had long, flowing hair – unlike me. I recall being so excited to get a Jheri curl (don't laugh!), thinking that it would Americanize me. But a Jheri curl on a low-cut afro leads to hair that sticks up, not long and flowing hair like my mom's.

It was also the year I realized that I was darker than my siblings. I began to notice that they looked cuter than me because they looked more American than me. My brother was in the 6th grade of the same school, but his experience was completely different from mine. He wasn't experiencing any of this to my knowledge. My sister was in elementary school so my guess is the kids weren't as mean as the middle-schoolers yet. Plus, she had always been beautiful (and she still is).

As a result of all the creative things the kids found to say to me like "you're so black" (most of these were other black kids, by the way), I became creative in my blend game, i.e., my attempt to go unnoticed. I found different routes to take to my classes. I would rush to my next class before my taunters made it to the hallway. I worked on my accent (and probably sounded like a hot mess) so that if I had to speak in class, I would not stand out. Then, after a long, tough day at school, I would go home, run to the mirror, and try to find anything that looked good about me. Instead, I found other things wrong, like the gap between my front teeth or my big nose or my huge forehead.

After that school year, my family moved from the apartment we lived in to a rented house in a more diverse neighborhood. Moving to a different neighborhood didn't seem to fix anything. We may have moved away from the source of my pain, but the damage to my young soul had already been done. I continued to carry around the belief that I wasn't worthy because I was ugly.

In my new school, I still avoided making eye contact every time I passed by a group of boys because, inevitably, one would make fun of me and the others would laugh or join in. I avoided certain routes altogether. I made friends with the outliers, those who were made fun of and didn't fit in. I focused on my grades until kids started making fun of that, too. (Being called an ugly, fat nerd somehow felt worse than just being called fat and ugly.) The day that one of my classmates (a skater dude) found out my age and began announcing that I was the youngest in my class, the desire to be accepted (or at least to blend in) was so strong that I hit an all-time low and started to get bad grades in my classes intentionally.

Being back in the U.S. was not turning out to be what I had expected. I lost my excitement and joy each time I got made fun of for being African, for having dark skin, for having an accent, for being a nerd, or for being young. It caused me to hate myself. It made me stay silent in class. It made me hang my head low as I walked down the hallway to class, especially if I saw a group of guys hanging together.

As a result of this experience, I went into hiding, and I didn't emerge for many years. It affected me for many years, well beyond college. I wanted to fit in so badly that I learned to hide in ways that I didn't even realize. I couldn't change my skin, but I made sure I changed the other things about me that made me stick out. I learned to dumb myself down so that I wouldn't stand out academically. I changed my accent. I did not share my thoughts and opinions in certain settings and accepted what others said, even if internally I didn't agree. I changed my name (not legally), introducing myself to new acquaintances as Emmy (which they pronounced as Amy, and I ran with it), instead of Emem. Even at home, I learned to hide my true self and mastered the art of keeping secrets from my family.

Why this book?

I decided to write this book to help those of you who are also hiding. The details of your shadow story may be different from mine, but the need for you to remove the mask is the same. It is time to give yourself permission to step out spiritually, emotionally, and mentally and live as your authentic self.

My mission through this book is to inspire you to show up boldly as the authentic you. You deserve the transformation that will follow. You are going to experience some resistance, and it won't feel comfortable along the way, but it will be worth it in the end.

So, here's why I'm writing this book:

- Because you have a gift (heck, several gifts, even if you don't know what they are yet), and the longer you wear the mask, the longer you deprive the world of your God-given gifts

- Because I have firsthand knowledge and experience of what an unfulfilled life feels like, but I also now know what finding fulfillment feels like

- Because I believe you have more in you than to merely stay stuck in the shadows while your gifts waste away

- Because I believe that showing up as the real you and using your gifts to positively impact the lives of others is the cure for that restless discontentment that you can't shake

- Because it is time for you to stop hiding behind your job, your family, your comfort zone, and your excuses and do the things you know you've been called to do.

I want you to come out of your shell. I want you to overcome your past, reclaim your voice, and live (shine) your light. I want you to let go of the things that have kept you stuck and stagnant and live the life God created you to live.

SELAH MOMENT

Pause for a moment and reflect.

1. What is your shadow story?

_____

_____

_____

_____

_____

_____

_____

_____

_____

_____

2. Can you recall when you first withdrew into the false version(s) of yourself? List the details surrounding your withdrawal.

_____

_____

_____

_____

_____

_____

_____

3. Are there certain people in your life with whom you can be your true self? What is it about them that makes you feel safe to reveal the true you?

_____

_____

_____

_____

_____

_____

_____

2

SHIFT HAPPENS

If outside validation is your only source of nourishment, you will hunger for the rest of your life.

- Unknown

We live in an age where there is an increased focus on inclusion and diversity. Many organizations have put in place teams that are dedicated to making sure employees feel included and their differences understood and accepted. In spite of this trend, recent studies show that employees are still hiding certain aspects of their authentic selves to fit in at work.

Hiding our authentic selves shows up in our different roles and relationships, such as our relationships as spouses, friends, and employees. We look for ways to shrink ourselves to appear less than we truly are, or we camouflage who we are to blend in with others.

Camouflaging is a survival technique, a protective strategy used by the military and certain organisms (e.g., chameleons) to disguise themselves and blend in with their surroundings. The purpose is to hide from the threat of an enemy by masking your identity and location. Whether we hide by wearing masks, by shrinking, or by camouflaging, the result is that we silence our voice and turn off our light, which can manifest in subtle ways such as continuing to stay at a job that is draining you physically, emotionally, and mentally or continuing in relationships long past their expiration date.

The interesting thing is that it is more difficult to pretend to be someone else than to be yourself. It's also detrimental. The impact of hiding is not only damaging to your sense of self, it affects everyone around you. It might feel safe, but it is actually very harmful. You lose precious time out of your life living like a shadow of yourself; time you can never get back.

Living as a fake version of yourself can feel like you're being gracious, i.e., you feel that you are helping other people feel good about themselves. Even if that were true (and it's not), you are hurting yourself. And if you have to hide who you are so they can feel good about themselves at your expense, how does that really help them?

You are good enough to stand out as yourself. Do it to show others what is possible. Shining your light does not take away from theirs. Stay humble but shine!

Turning Point

I woke up one day, and I wondered where the past thirteen years of my life had gone. By this time, I was a mother, and life did not look like what I had thought it would look like at that stage of my life. What happened to the person that had started law school with big dreams and aspirations to leave her mark in the world? No matter how big my dreams were, nothing would come of them if I did not show up as my authentic self.

While I was still pondering where the years had gone and assessing what I had managed to achieve in life, my mother passed away suddenly while away on an international trip. My world fell apart, and my family and I were devastated. Before her trip, she had recorded the episodes of some of her favorite shows that she would miss while she was gone. She expressed that she was looking forward to watching them when she returned. She never made it back to watch those shows.

Months prior to her trip, I had promised her that within three years (God willing) I would buy her dream home for her as gratitude for all she had done for my siblings and me. I never got to fulfill my promise, but God had a better home for her than I could ever give her.

As traumatic as her death was, it served as a catalyst that God used at that time to jumpstart my journey out of that stuck place where I held on to the past and hid my voice. It forced me to understand how short life really is. She made plans to return and watch her shows but never returned, and that thought haunted me in my own life. She had finished her race, but if God called me home next, could the same be said of me?

Another catalyst was the fact that my sons were now at an age where they noticed everything I said and did, including when I suppressed my authentic self. I knew that I could not expect them to show up authentically in their own lives if I didn't model for them what it looked like to do so.

It was a period of growth for me. I began to pay attention to and be intentional with my words and my actions. I made bolder decisions concerning my life and what I would and would not accept. At any moment, life could end, and I did not want to have regrets. I grew in my relationship with God, and I realized that even if I hid from everyone else, I could never hide from Him. He saw me completely – the public me, the private me, and the hidden me – and He loved me as I was.

God also opened my eyes to see the need for having coaches and mentors in my life. I had never really believed that having a life coach was anything worth investing in, but many of the major breakthroughs and successes God has allowed me to receive have been because I sought out amazing coaches. They affirmed me and caused me to see the blocks that were keeping me from being fully present in my own life and causing me to stay stuck. This has played a tremendous role in my ability to boldly show up authentically and unapologetically. And, while I can't say that I don't have moments when the less-than-enough me tries to come out, I am now well-equipped to handle those moments.

The transformation in my life has been phenomenal. When I decided to leave the shadows behind, it felt like a heavy weight had been lifted off of me. That weight was the weight of being someone else and not being happy with the person that I was. It was the weight of not understanding why people would make fun of the person that I truly was. With that weight gone, I was able to go back to the dreams that I had tucked away on a shelf somewhere and allow myself to dream again and to pursue those dreams. I began to participate in things that lit up my soul.

And, that is what I want you to take away from this book. I want your soul to light up. I want you to succeed, to excel, to move on to the next level, to pass. Yes, pass. Each letter in the word P-A-S-S has a meaning, so let's take a look at each one of these individually.

Pursue Your Dreams

As a kid, I enjoyed acting, singing, writing, and speaking. I would make up songs and teach them to my siblings. I would write poems and share them with anyone who would listen. I loved acting in school plays, and often got the difficult task of being the narrator, which meant memorizing lots of lines. I loved it! In high school one day, I saw an announcement for auditions for the next school play, which would be the story of Helen Keller. I was so excited and summoned up the courage to audition. (I hadn't auditioned for a play in the four years since my family had been back to the U.S.). A friend and I decided to sign up for auditions together.

On the day of the auditions, the theater department teacher told my friend and me that we would not be auditioning for the role of Annie or Helen because it was unrealistic for either of us to play those characters since neither of them was black. Instead, we would audition for the role of a maid, and he would even create an extra part so that we could both be in the play.

On opening night of the play, my mom came to watch it, and afterwards expressed her disappointment at the roles we had been given to play, and I understood why. It was a play, a drama, so even if the characters in Helen Keller's story were not black, anybody could have played any of the characters, regardless of skin color. Looking back, I wish I had not taken the part, but I loved acting and wanted to be in the school play. So, I pretended not to be bothered about the role.

That experience left me with more doubts about my worth. I was mad at myself for allowing others to see how excited I was to audition for a role in that play. I was embarrassed that, after showing my excitement, I ended up with a role as a maid. I think I also started limiting my expectations subconsciously and settling for the "less-than-enough" mindset.

For years after that, I ignored my creative side and the things I enjoyed doing, especially in light of the fact that my dad wanted me to become a doctor. I still really loved writing and speaking and acting and singing, but I set all of those things on the shelf and focused on school and afterward, career and motherhood. I ended up becoming a lawyer (not a doctor) and focused on doing well in my profession.

I was good at what I did, but I was not fulfilled. The more I tried to suppress the things I enjoyed, the more they haunted my thoughts at the most random times. And so, after many years, I decided to stop suppressing my dreams and start pursuing them. I brought those old dreams and desires off the shelf and made the decision to finally show up as my authentic self. It was not easy because I worried about what family members would think or what fellow attorneys would say. "You're doing what? Singing?"

I thought that I was too old to release my own music. Who would listen? And if I wrote a book, who would want to read what I had to say? I wish I could tell you that I overcame those limiting thoughts immediately, but it's not true. It took time and lots of work in the area of mastering my mindset. But, I can tell you that I have released a CD (serendipitously titled *Rebirth*); I can tell you that I have become a published author, and I can tell you that I now get invited to speak (and sing) on various stages. And, the beauty of all of this is that I get to do these in furtherance of my ultimate goal, which is to have a life of impact. Imagine if I had not learned to let go of the concern of what my fellow lawyers and other professionals would think of me if I pursued those things? What if I let those dreams stay hidden? All of the above is to say that I want you to pursue your dreams as well.

Appreciate Your Identity

Understanding and appreciating your unique identity is important. It provides meaning and purpose for our lives. When you know who you are and *whose* you are, things change. You are not jealous of other people, and you can celebrate their successes without feeling left behind. You don't allow what others call you to hold you down.

Look at David in the Bible.

- His identity was challenged by his brothers. (His older brother Eliab called him proud and rude.)

- His identity was challenged by King Saul who said he was just a youth and not enough to defeat the mighty Goliath.

- His identity was challenged by Goliath who cursed him and promised to feed him to the animals.

Let's not forget that earlier in his story he was overlooked by his father and brothers when Samuel was looking for the next king. But David did not shrink because he knew his identity, and he knew the identity of the God to whom he belonged. When you know who God is, you know who you are. When you know who you are, you can come out from the dark and shine your light. The scars of past hurtful words and actions no longer have the power to keep you trapped in the shadows.

SELAH MOMENT

Pause for a moment and reflect.

1. What lies have you been listening to or telling yourself? What have you allowed yourself to believe?

_____

_____

_____

_____

_____

_____

_____

_____

_____

_____

2. Now, write a truth to counter each of those lies.

_____

_____

_____

_____

_____

_____

_____

_____

_____

_____

_____

_____

_____

3. What does the Bible say about your
   identity? Write it in a letter to yourself.
   Write in a voice as if you were talking to
   someone you love very much.

_____

_____

_____

_____

_____

_____

_____

_____

_____

_____

_____

_____

_____

_____

_____

Separate Yourself

You are not for everybody, and everybody is not for you. Everybody is not going to like you, and that is a blessing and not a curse. Detox your life from those who want you to show up as less than you are before they accept you in their circle. If they can't handle the greatness in you, then *they* need an adjustment, not you. The world needs the authentic you.

Besides, not everyone in your circle is in your corner. When you know those who are not in your corner, life becomes far less complicated. Remember Judas Iscariot? As one of the twelve disciples, he was in Jesus' circle. But clearly, he was not in Jesus' corner.

When you show up authentically, you will grow, but your circle will shrink. Those circles were not real anyway; after all, you made it into some of them because you were not showing up as the real you. Separate yourself from those circles that hinder your ability to thrive. You can start right now to prepare your mind to be okay with that. Do you think that God is interested in working through someone who cares more about what people will say over than what He says?

SELAH MOMENT

Pause for a moment and reflect.

1. Who do you need to let go of? Who is in your circle but not in your corner?

_____

_____

_____

_____

_____

_____

Shine Your Light

Once you know and appreciate who you are and you let go of those who hold your authentic self down, it's now time to shine. Shining does not require that you dim someone else's light. It means you step out from the shadows and begin to make the impact God created you to make. Listen, hiding is selfish. Playing small is selfish. It does not glorify God, and it does not serve humanity. And you are not a selfish person. You are someone who wants to serve God with what He has given you. So shine – for Jesus. Come out of hiding so that you can be a spotlight for God.

God won't get the glory by you staying in the shadows.

It's Time

It's time to PASS.

It's time to free yourself of the fear of what other people think of you.

It's time to accept yourself and show up as your true self.

It's time to come out from behind the shadows of others' expectations and step into your power.

It's time to find your voice and use it.

It's time to own the truth that you are a specially created person with as much a right as anyone else to live as your authentic self.

It's time to forgive yourself of the mistakes you've made on the journey to becoming you.

It's time to recognize who you truly are in God's eyes.

It's time to jump, despite those fears that have kept you stuck and stagnant.

It's time for you to be YOU.

What Happens When You Show Up Authentically?

When you begin to show up boldly and authentically as your true self, transformation is inevitable. You begin to feel seen, heard and genuinely appreciated, not just by others but by yourself. And that is a wonderful feeling!

You no longer dumb yourself down or dim your light just to suit the desires of others. You know who you are, and you are comfortable being yourself. You stop looking for outside sources to complete and validate you.

You find fulfillment because you stop accepting a mediocre life and start pursuing your own vision, no longer merely reluctantly accepting the visions of others.

Your words and actions are congruent with your beliefs and values.

You feel liberated as you experience less anxiety and stress because you no longer have to impersonate who others expect you to be. No longer are you bound by the fear of other people's judgments of you.

You start to attract people who are well-matched with your true self and release those who are not.

You start living again. You take control of your life and are no longer content to sit on the sidelines of your own life.

You realize the value that you have to offer.

You begin to make your own dreams a priority (even those dreams you thought you were too old to achieve) and start moving in the direction of your desires.

Imagine the difference you could make if you were able to create work you love and get generously compensated for it. How would your life change if you could have deeper and more supportive and rewarding relationships, where you were free to be yourself? What would it feel like to walk into any setting and not immediately feel the need to dumb yourself down?

Remember those big dreams that you once had? It's not too late for you. Stop suppressing yourself. Open up and fully express those gifts in you. Take off the mask, stand up tall, and come out of the shadows. You were not meant to live life as a shrunken version of yourself to please anyone else. God is calling you to rise up. Rise up and do what He has given you to do. You do not need a nod of approval from anyone; you only need to hear from God.

3

———

TAKE OFF THE MASK

If you can't be your authentic self, you're connecting with the wrong people. They're wasting your time and holding you back.

- Dr. Henry Cloud

Did you ever try chasing your shadow as a child or try to make it disappear? As much as you tried to shake it, your shadow followed you around like a companion. Even when you didn't notice it, your shadow was there. It did what you did, moved when you moved, and stuck with you wherever you went. It would sometimes appear as a shorter version of you and other times a taller version, but it was not you.

While a shadow indicates that there is light present, a shadow is not light. The area covered by the shadow is dark and is formed when an object blocks the light. What are you allowing to block your light?

In the shadows, you constantly seek the approval of others. You are so concerned about what other people think that you often find yourself in a state of anxiety and discontent. You operate in a zone of frequent dissatisfaction about your life and envy of the lives of others. You are frustrated because you are not living in your purpose, and the years are rapidly passing you by.

When you are hidden in the shadows, whether your shadow or someone (or something) else's, you are believing lies about yourself. You believe that you don't fit in. You believe that you're not worthy. You believe that you're too much. You believe that you're useless. You believe that you're not enough or that you're not qualified. You are living a life less than the life God intends for you to live. You are not fulfilling the destiny you were born to live.

I believed all kinds of lies about myself. It held me down and kept me bound. While I believed that God could use anybody to do His will, I didn't believe that He could use me in any significant way because I was damaged goods and unworthy. I became what others expected of me and made poor decisions concerning myself. I put aside the big dreams I once had.

The more I stayed in the shadows, the more miserable I became. I stayed silent in situations where I should have spoken up. I became envious each time I saw others doing things that I wanted to do, things that were part of the dreams I had tucked away. Until I finally accepted and owned who I was, the gifts God deposited in me stayed trapped inside of me where they served nobody.

It is draining to try to be who you are not. You lose your joy as you constantly compare yourself to others, pursuing their acceptance over pursuing your dreams. You find yourself constantly feeling unsatisfied with your life.

Signs that you are Hiding

You might be in hiding if (this is not an exhaustive list):

- You are constantly trying to please others.

- You have resigned yourself to remaining at your unfulfilling job just because it pays the bills.

- You behave a certain way whenever you are around certain groups of people.

- You bite your tongue when you know you need to speak up for what's right.

- You have the opportunity to contribute, but you hold yourself back so that others won't feel intimidated.

- You commit yourself to things you don't enjoy.

- You participate in activities that don't line up with your personal beliefs.

You will never become the person God created you to become if you pretend to be who you are not. And as you may have heard it said, God will not bless the fake version of you. And I know you want all of the blessings that God has for you.

By denying who you are, you hurt yourself deeply and keep yourself from getting to the level you secretly want to get to. It keeps you stagnant and makes you feel irrelevant. It causes you to put walls around your purpose. You believe the lie that your true self is not enough, and you continue people-pleasing attempting to find significance. You feel empty inside. It can make you resentful and envious as you watch others fully living their lives while you're on the sidelines of your own life with someone else narrating your story.

When you seek your value in the opinions of others, you find yourself out of alignment with the life that God designed exclusively for you. You will never become the person God intended for you to become if continue fearing what "they" will think, say, or do. You will never be satisfied because you keep trying to be who you are not, and it never feels like enough. And by treating yourself as less than enough, you give others permission to do the same.

What is causing you to stay in the shadows, afraid to shine your light, afraid of showing up as the real you? What lies have you believed about yourself? It's time to overcome the lies. The more you immerse yourself in the truth and the more you absorb the word and uncover what God says about you, the more you can bring the lies to light. When you figure out what's keeping you from showing up, you'll be able to begin releasing those old beliefs and move forward into the light.

Your story might be different from mine, but the underlying reason we all hide is the same: Fear. You may have retreated into the shadows because of a painful event in your past, but the reason you continue to stay there is because of fear. That fear can stem from a past experience where approval was withheld from you, or you were criticized by people who mattered to you. It could stem from that time you didn't receive the reassurance that you needed, which led to you feeling insecure and afraid to reveal your true self.

Or maybe you're afraid that who you are will be rejected and ridiculed, or you're afraid of being judged. Or afraid that you will fail and afraid of how it will make you look to others. That fear of failing, of falling, is a trap that keeps you from living out your best life. It keeps you from taking a chance on yourself, on your ideas, and on others. It keeps you from truly living. Yes, it hurts when we fail, but regret for never taking a chance will end up hurting even more.

In my own life, if I had continued to stay hidden and cooped up in my shell, there were so many things that I would never have done, things that have not only benefited me but also those around me. I would never have gotten remarried. I would never have continued to try to have children after having multiple stillbirths/miscarriages. I would never have recorded and released my own CD. I would not have written this book or shared my story to inspire others. I would not be living the life I was created by God to live.

There are other reasons that fear rears its head. Maybe you're afraid the real you might intimidate people. Or you're afraid of success. Perhaps you fear that it's too late for you, that your time has passed, so why bother showing up? Or you're afraid that you've spent so much time hiding who you are that you won't be able to figure out who you really are anymore. Or it could be that you fear that people will judge you if you show them who you truly are.

It is worth repeating that you will continue to be unhappy and envious of others as you watch them live if you stay in the shadows. Whether you hide or whether you shine, people are going to keep living their own lives. And at the end of the day, do you really want to be that person that is full of regrets because you did not live up to your potential?

You might still be thinking, *But seriously, what if I fail?* Let me ask you: What if you do? What if that "failure" works together for your good? What if you succeed beyond your wildest dreams?

SELAH MOMENT

Pause for a moment and reflect.

1. How has hiding from your authentic self seemed to serve you?

_____

_____

_____

_____

_____

_____

_____

_____

2. How will it serve you to let go of the fear of showing up?

_____

_____

_____

_____

_____

_____

_____

_____

3. What is possible when the authentic you shows up?

_____

_____

_____

_____

_____

_____

_____

_____

_____

_____

_____

_____

_____

_____

_____

The remaining chapters are designed to guide you toward breakthrough in overcoming your past, reclaiming your voice, and living your light. As you go through the reading and exercises on the next few pages, I encourage you to be candid with yourself and don't censor yourself. There has already been too much of that by you and by others.

Take your time to reflect before you respond. Don't rush this part. The results you get will depend on you, so lean in completely.

If you are a music lover like me, I have included two playlists you can listen to while doing the exercises. Or, you can listen to them any time you need a reminder of who you are. One playlist has more mid-tempo to up-tempo songs, and the other includes slower, more reflective songs. Both are available in the Bonus section of this book.

4

_____

OVERCOME YOUR PAST

If we want to create a different future,
we must have the courage to look at the past.

- Dan B. Allender

Negative events from our past affect our present and could affect our future negatively unless we recognize them and do the work required to overcome them. To overcome the past, we are going to journey back, but we will not stay there. This is not going to be easy. It will require work, but it is work that will be worth it. Do you really want to come to the end of your life and wonder what you did with who you are and where you are and what God gave you?

When we bring up the past, there is often something we are seeking or needing in the present. It is usually an indicator that we are feeling similar emotions as we did as a result of that past experience. At that moment, you might feel hurt or insecure, misunderstood, or unloved, just like you felt before. Ask God to intervene and destroy the grip that your past has on you. Ask Him to show you how you can begin moving forward, and what lessons He wants you to learn from the past. God is bigger than your past and can transform your pain into healing and wisdom.

If you feel led to, open up about your past with other people who are struggling with similar issues. This can bring healing and hope, not just to them, but to you as well.

What occurred to start you on this journey of shutting down emotionally or seeking the approval of others? For some people, these occurrences are from childhood. For others, they might have happened in adulthood. However, if you dig really deep, you will probably find something in your childhood that was the trigger or catalyst.

I began this book by sharing about my middle school experience, but as I dug deeper, I remembered an experience from when I was around six years old. It was really the first time that I realized that I was different from the other kids because they pointed it out to me. We were living in England at the time, and my mom had threaded my hair, a style that was common in Nigeria. The kids asked why I had spiders on my head. Then they asked other questions I did not understand at the time, about whether or not I looked different from them underneath my clothes. Needless to say, I did not enjoy the questions or the description that they used to describe my hairstyle. Thinking back, this was probably when I started to crave the safety of blending in rather than standing out.

Some examples of triggering events that I have seen, heard of, or experienced include being teased due to your family's financial situation, being sexually abused by a family member, being made fun of because of something unique about yourself, having a verbally or physically abusive parent, a teacher saying something negative and hurtful to you, having a narcissistic person in your life (parent, significant other, etc.), having a parent who is an addict, having a family member die or walk out on your family, not feeling loved or supported by someone you relied on for affection, just to name a few.

SELAH MOMENT

Pause for a moment and reflect.

1. Write down all triggering events that you can remember.

_____
_____
_____
_____
_____
_____
_____
_____
_____
_____
_____
_____
_____
_____

2. Which events from your past still affect different areas of your life today? Don't try to minimize or suppress your feelings. Acknowledge and accept your emotions, feel them, but don't dwell on them. Resist the temptation to remain stuck in self-pity or hurt.

_____

_____

_____

_____

_____

_____

_____

_____

_____

3. Who were the people involved in causing the pain?

_____

_____

_____

_____

_____

_____

_____

_____

_____

_____

_____

_____

_____

_____

4. What are the emotions you feel when you think about these painful events and the people involved?

_____

_____

_____

_____

_____

_____

_____

_____

_____

_____

5. What are the triggers that take you back to this painful place? Is it a song? A day of the year? A certain environment?

_____

_____

_____

_____

_____

_____

_____

_____

_____

_____

_____

6. List ways that you plan to remove or avoid the triggers that can be avoided or removed. How will you respond differently to those that cannot be avoided or removed? Coming up with a plan ahead of time will help you to be better prepared for the triggering event.

_____

_____

_____

_____

_____

_____

_____

_____

_____

_____

_____

7. Understand that, while you cannot rewrite what happened to you, you can change how you view what happened and how you respond to it going forward. In what ways can you change your response to what happened?

_____

_____

_____

_____

_____

_____

_____

_____

_____

_____

_____

_____

_____

_____

8. Forgive even if there has not been an apology. Don't wait for the person(s) who hurt you to acknowledge or apologize for their role in your pain. Unforgiveness takes power away from you and puts it in their hands. Ask God for the grace and strength to let them go. Then, go through the mental process of releasing and forgiving them. Who do you need to forgive? Use the lines below to write out a forgiveness statement for each person you need to forgive. For example, I forgive (insert name) for (what you are forgiving them for).

_____

_____

_____

_____

_____

_____

_____

_____

9. What are the positives in your life right now?

_____

10. How will your life change (relationships, career, mindset, etc.) when you finally let go of the past?

_____

11. Other than you, who will benefit once you
     let go of the past?

5

RECLAIM YOUR VOICE

For the soul-wounded woman. Your healed voice is my favorite sound. Your hurts, they walk right into our hearts; but your story of healing – that can change lives. Never be afraid to find and use your voice.

- Jo Ann Fore

We are not born quiet. Children are experts at using their natural voices. They don't struggle with "keeping it real." Babies come out screaming, and while they might not know how to say any words, they do know how (and are not afraid) to freely express their emotions when they are upset, scared, or happy. However, along the way, something alters the way we see ourselves, and it affects our belief in our right to be heard in the world. We become aware that expressing what we think and feel can have negative consequences. This awareness causes us to modify or suppress our voices. We modify our voices for a myriad of reasons, such as to be accepted, to blend in, to be polite, or to be liked. Some of us modified our voices due to a loss or some other type of trauma.

The Role of Culture

Culture can affect how we suppress our voices in many ways, regardless of where we are in the world.

- Women learn that they are supposed to talk softly; otherwise, they are considered too aggressive, so you rarely speak up.

- Men learn that they are not supposed to discuss or express their emotions; otherwise, they are considered weak, so they silently suffer through their emotions.

- Children learn that they are supposed to be seen and not heard, so they bring that voiceless identity into adulthood. Their views are disregarded, and their ideas are discredited by adults, which sends the message that their voice is not important. They learn that there is no point in speaking up or speaking out.

- You are not supposed to express anger as an African-American woman, or you'll be labeled as an "angry black woman," so you stay silent.

- You learn that you're not supposed to toot your own horn, so you downplay yourself.

Other Reasons for Suppressing Our Voices

Suppressing your voice is not limited to those times when someone told you to be quiet. In the first chapter, I shared with you how it was humiliating to be outed as the youngest in my class while making good grades. I stopped pushing myself so hard because that was yet another way that I was different from everyone else, and being different had its consequences.

We stay silent because of something said by people in our circle – parents, teachers, family members, friends, co-workers, bosses, and clergy. We stay silent because of things we hear on television or read in books. We stay silent in our relationships because we don't want to rock the boat. We stay silent because we think we're being diplomatic. Are we really being diplomatic or are we just people-pleasers?

I remember a conversation I had one day in 2015 with a coworker. I was trying to share my view on something, but she would cut me off every few words. After three attempts, I stopped trying because I had decided a long time ago that whenever that happened, it meant that I was not supposed to say what I planned to say. After I stopped trying, she finally asked me what I had wanted to say, and I shared with her my rationale for not needing to share it anymore. She basically told me that my rationale was hogwash and that being interrupted could also mean that other people (herself included) were just conversation hogs and not the best listeners, and that I should no longer let that way of thinking keep me silent. Here I thought that I was being strong by making a sacrifice (my voice for theirs) when really I was suppressing my voice.

Many times you may know exactly what you want to say and what you have to say has the potential to change a situation or a life, but you hold yourself back from saying it. The result of your silence impacts not just you, but all of us collectively. When we believe that our voices do not matter, we don't bother to vote because we believe that our votes and our voices don't matter. Our silence perpetuates the culture of silence (we end up seeing it in our children), and it hinders our collective progress.

If you have lost your voice, it's time to reclaim it. It's time to reconnect with your authentic voice. Your voice matters. Losing your voice is practically the same as losing your identity, and we've already discussed the importance of your identity in Chapter 2. Remember that saying what you want to say, how you want to say it, is not about taking power from someone else but about also giving power to yourself.

Whether you lost your voice due to a life-shattering event, or whether it was due to something less traumatic, like the culture you grew up in, reclaiming your voice is necessary, and it is doable. Once again, I invite you to do the exercises below, to begin the transformation work necessary to recover your authentic voice. Take some time and sit with the memories involved in answering the questions. Don't stop them. Do whatever helps you work through the process, e.g., listen to music, cry, journal, share with a loved one, go for a walk or run – whatever works best for you.

SELAH MOMENT

Pause for a moment and reflect.

1. When was your authentic voice first silenced? Describe everything about it: your age, who was involved, what happened, etc. Write the events that unfolded that made you feel that you should be quiet.

_____

_____

_____

_____

_____

_____

_____

_____

_____

_____

_____

_____

_____

_____

_____

_____

_____

2. When was the last time you felt like you could express yourself fully without hesitation or fear?

_____

_____

_____

_____

_____

3. Observe your daily interactions. In the environments listed below, do you feel free to speak up or do you stop yourself from speaking up? Explain why or why not.

At work:

_____

_____

_____

_____

_____

_____

At home:

_____

_____

_____

_____

_____

_____

In your relationships outside of home:

_____

_____

_____

_____

_____

_____

_____

_____

4. Who or what makes you feel unheard?

_____

_____

_____

_____

_____

5. How has being unheard impacted your ability to listen to and hear other people?

_____

_____

_____

_____

_____

_____

_____

6. When does/did your voice feel most expressed?

_____
_____
_____
_____
_____

7. When does/did your voice feel most suppressed?

_____
_____
_____
_____
_____

8. When does/did your voice feel most empowered?

_____
_____
_____
_____
_____

9. When does/did your voice feel most overpowered?

_____
_____
_____
_____
_____

Vocal Exercises

Over the next few days and weeks, find 5–10 minutes a day to practice vocalizing in private. Make all kinds of sounds—sing, shout, whistle, and most especially, talk. Let sound flow freely from you. Practice talking at differing volumes. Practice talking in various tones. Practice saying no to people to whom you've always said yes when you really wanted to say no. Practice speaking up.

Record yourself doing these vocal exercises. Listen to the playback and honestly assess how you sound. Each day, try to sound more comfortable and confident than the previous day. Initially, you might feel silly or uncomfortable but push through. The idea is to get used to hearing your voice in various ways in private so that you will be ready to speak out in public when opportunities arise.

Look for opportunities to speak up. Start small and grow from there. For example, you can share your opinion or one of your ideas to your colleague or boss or even at the next office meeting. You can speak up (politely, of course) when someone says something distasteful or hurtful. You can tell that friend no when she invites you out for lunch, and you really don't want to go.

Give yourself permission to speak. Listen to yourself. And don't let those who are not listening overshadow those who are.

6

SHINE YOUR LIGHT

Let your light shine today, and let
your personality blossom, too.
You don't have to be a people-pleaser,
just a people-lover.

- Beth Moore

Although shining your light can be overwhelming, it's one of the greatest gifts you can give yourself. It's time to walk in full expression of the gifts God has placed in you. In this chapter, we walk through steps and tools that'll help you on your journey from the shadows toward living your light.

You have the power to take back your power. You *can* live as your authentic self. You can overcome your past and reclaim your voice. You can shine your light brightly. I know because I've done it and I now have the privilege of coaching other beautiful souls to do the same. And it really is a privilege because what they have kept hidden for so long is pure brilliance. The journey with them from the shadows to the light is rewarding and fulfilling, not just for them but for me as well.

God has a unique path planned for you so your journey will not look like that of anyone else's. When you take these steps, you allow yourself the opportunity to fulfill the destiny and purpose God has for you and to live out the passion He has placed in you. You allow yourself to break the chains of the past that still have you bound and to shine your light. And by doing so, you model for others who are hiding what it looks like to shine so they can give themselves permission to do the same.

God has gifted you differently and uniquely from anyone else. You add value in your own special way. Stop pretending that greatness doesn't live in you. Stop masquerading and masking your genius. Stop hiding from your gift. You have permission to be great.

It is time to come out of your shell, take off the mask, and rise from the shadows. However you choose to phrase it, it is time. Do it and experience a renewed life, a rebirth. Stop giving into the lies. Stop living someone else's life. Stop dumbing yourself down. You have a beautiful brilliance based on your own unique combination of knowledge, wisdom, passions, skillset, calling, gifts, and experience. You are the only one that can offer your brilliance into the world.

So what if they whisper? So what if they laugh? So what if they mock you? So what if they exclude you? You will be too much for some people, and for others, you will not be enough. Keep your eyes on the One who created you. Do the work below to get started on your journey to get your light back.

Dream God-Sized Dreams

Permit yourself to dream big, scary dreams. The dreams that scare us the most are usually the dreams we are meant to pursue. And they typically produce the most growth and expansion in our lives. Envision your life in six months. Envision your life next year. What are you doing? One of the things we do in our Vision Workshops is to take a deep look into our goals and allow ourselves to dream big. There's something powerful that happens when you dream God-sized dreams because you know that those dreams can only come to pass with God.

SELAH MOMENT

Pause for a moment and reflect.

Now that you're taking this journey towards light and coming out of your shadow let's also take a look at those dreams that you have put on hold for the longest time. Rediscover those things that light you up, that make you happy. If you can't figure out what those are, take a look at what lit you up when you were a child.

1. At what point in your life were you the happiest?

_____

_____

_____

_____

_____

2. What was going on in your life during that time? What were you doing? Who were you with? What about those things made you happy?

_____

_____

_____

_____

_____

_____

3. Do those things and those people you listed above still give you joy? Explain.

_____

_____

_____

_____

_____

4. What activities or environments make you feel the most alive?

_____

_____

_____

_____

_____

_____

_____

5. What activities or environments make you feel the most exhausted?

_____

_____

_____

_____

_____

_____

6. If you could do anything for the rest of your life, what would that be? Why? Don't hold back and don't censor yourself.

_____
_____
_____
_____
_____
_____
_____

7. What do you enjoy doing, even if you aren't getting paid to do it?

_____
_____
_____
_____
_____
_____

8. Go over all of your answers in this section. What trend do you observe? What big dreams did you come up with?

_____
_____
_____
_____
_____
_____
_____

9. If the dreams you wrote above do not really scare you, go back to the drawing board. Write BIGGER dreams below.

_____

_____

_____

_____

_____

_____

_____

Establish Your Identity

Who are you? Maybe you've spent so much time hiding your true self that you don't even remember who you are. To discover or rediscover your identity, ask yourself the questions in the Identity Exercise below, and write your answers. Dig deep and be intentional with your responses. Feel free to use a separate journal or additional paper if more space is required.

1. Who am I?

_____

_____

_____

_____

_____

_____

_____

_____

_____

2. Who does God say I am, i.e., what is my identity in Christ? If you've wondered what your purpose is, then knowing your identity will help you discover your purpose.

_____

_____

_____

_____

_____

_____

_____

_____

_____

3. What traits do I possess? What makes me stand out?

_____

_____

_____

_____

_____

_____

_____

_____

4. What are all the different roles I have in my life?

_____

_____

_____

_____

_____

5. What do I stand for?

_____

_____

_____

_____

_____

_____

_____

6. What are my core values?

_____

_____

_____

_____

_____

_____

_____

7. How do I want to be perceived?

_____

_____

_____

_____

_____

_____

8. How do I want to be remembered?

_____

_____

_____

_____

_____

9. What kind of people do I want to associate with?

_____

_____

_____

_____

_____

10. What are the qualities I want to attract and nurture in my life?

_____

_____

_____

_____

_____

_____

Now that you have identified who you are and what you stand for, it is time to figure out how to live in alignment with the real you.

11. Write about how you can begin to take action in alignment with your authentic self.

_____

_____

_____

_____

_____

_____

_____

_____

_____

12. What activities that bring me joy and make me feel alive at heart? Write them below and then begin to do them!

_____

_____

_____

_____

_____

_____

_____

_____

_____

_____

Show Yourself Some Love

Give yourself the love that you've been giving to other people. Give yourself the love that you've been seeking from other people. Be kind to yourself, not just to others. To love anyone else, you have to love yourself first. Make peace with yourself.

Love yourself enough to release the need for validation from anyone but God. Stop acting differently depending on who we are with. If you have friends who will not "invite you to the party" if you don't conform to their notions of worth, or if you don't look the part, then it's time to "throw your own party" and invite a better group of friends. Let go of other people's expectations and begin focusing on how you wish to be perceived.

Love yourself enough to let go of what others think of you. You will never be able to please everyone. In fact, you should never aim to please anyone. God has gifted you uniquely from anyone else. There is no other you on earth. God decided that He wanted someone with your qualities here on earth to represent Him, so He created you.

Love yourself enough to let go of the people who intentionally overlook or downplay your gift, who underestimate you, and who ignore and exclude you. Choose to forgive them and move on. Release any and all resentment against them. Don't become a co-participant with them. The harm was their fault. But allowing it to impact who you are today is yours.

Love yourself enough to let go of the past. By holding on to the past, you rob yourself of the ability to enjoy the beauty in the present or prepare for an amazing future. You cannot get that time back, but you have a say in your today and your tomorrow.

Declutter Your Soul

We just talked about loving yourself enough to let go of some things. What else are you holding on to? When we hold on to things that don't serve us, our lives become cluttered with dead weight, stuff that has no value and weighs us down and keeps us stuck. So again I ask, what else are you holding on to? It is time to let go.

- Let go of the distractions.

- Let go of the naysayers.

- Let go of the regrets.

- Let go of the shame.

- Let go of the pain.

- Let go of the habits.

- Let go of limiting mindsets.

- Let go, so that you can have room for what matters.

- Let go and open yourself up to what God has in store for you.

SELAH MOMENT

Pause for a moment and reflect.

What dead weight are you holding on to and need to let go of?

_____

_____

_____

_____

_____

_____

_____

_____

_____

_____

_____

_____

7

YOU'VE GOT THIS

You are one decision away from a completely different life.

- Mel Robbins

Your next level is ready for you, but you have to show up. Don't let it pass you by. You may not have a huge crowd cheering you on, but you don't need the crowd, you have God. And you have me.

I use my voice to help pull out the greatness that lies within you. I help prep you to step into your next level. I know what it's like to play small so that you can fit in and be welcomed. To let others take credit for your ideas so that you won't rock the boat, or be seen as doing too much. To dumb down your genius, even while knowing what you're capable of. To be different, yet wanting to be just like everyone else because you don't want to disrupt the scene. Cringing when you are praised publicly because you do not want attention but also being frustrated that the recognition for your output was given to the wrong person.

It's not going to be easy. Sometimes you're going to feel like running back to the comfort of the mask or the obscurity of the shadows. Some of those same people will still try to make you feel small or exclude you. There may even be moments that you wonder if God really called you to this new you and this new level. Yes, He did. Let me say that again: Yes, He did, so keep heading towards the light of your authentic self. Your brilliance is a gift from God to be used as a gift for others. It is time to shine.

What's next? I invite and encourage you to push through to breakthrough by doing the journal exercises in the previous chapters if you have not already done so. Now that you know what to do and why you need to do it, do not allow yourself to return to the same old, same old after reading this book and going through those exercises.

The world is waiting for your manifestation (see Romans 8:19). You owe it to yourself and to those who are in desperate need of what the real you has to offer, to come out from the shadows, reclaim your voice and shine your light. It's time to fully express those gifts that God has placed in you and to fulfill those dreams that He has given you.

If you would like additional support with discovering your purpose, I am available to serve you and walk this journey with you.

Email me at emem@ememwashington.com, and we can schedule a complimentary coaching call.

Finally, if you found this book helpful, it would mean a lot to me if you would leave a review on Amazon, and it would also help others find it easily and take the journey towards changing their lives as well.

I am rooting for you. You've got this!

BONUS RESOURCES

I have put together two bonus resources to help you on your journey to leaving the shadows behind or whenever you need to be reminded of how special you are.

The first bonus is a list of empowering songs further broken into two playlists. You can also listen to them while you go through the exercises in this book or during your regular quiet time moments. The first playlist contains upbeat and mid-tempo songs that you can listen to while doing chores or working out. The second playlist contains songs for when you are in a more meditative or reflective mood.

If you are reading a digital version of this book, click the links below to access the YouTube playlists. If you are reading the print version of this book, you can access the playlist by typing the links into your web browser of choice. This list is not exhaustive, and as I come across other songs that are a good fit, I will add them. If you have any suggestions, send them my way. Happy listening!

The second bonus is a list of verses from God's word that speak to how special you are and how God sees you. You can read this at any time, especially whenever you feel like running back to the false security of the shadows. A great exercise would be to journal what God speaks to your heart as you read each verse.

BONUS RESOURCE #1A
Mid-tempo and Up-tempo Playlist

Playlist Link: bit.ly/RisePlaylistUpbeat

Songs included in playlist:

1. Identity – Israel Houghton
2. Rise Up From the Shadows – The Afters
3. I Know Who I Am – Sinach
4. Identify – Joel Positive Murray
5. I Know Who I Am – Israel Houghton
6. Lovely – Hollyn
7. Flip the Page – Emem Washington (feat Godswriter)
8. Different Drum – Blanca
9. Unfinished – Mandisa
10. Gold – Britt Nicole
11. Ready or Not – Britt Nicole, featuring LeCrae
12. Turn Around – Glowreeyah
13. Something Beautiful – Tori Kelly
14. Searchin' (On and On) – Emem Washington
15. Who I Am – Blanca
16. God Girl – Jamie Grace
17. Scars to Your Beautiful – Alessia Cara
18. Not Backing Down – Blanca

BONUS RESOURCE #1B

Quiet Time List – Meditative and Reflective Playlist

Playlist Link: bit.ly/RisePlaylistMeditative

Songs included in playlist:

1. Beautiful – Mercyme
2. He Knows My Name – Maranatha
3. He Knows My Name – Francesca Battistelli
4. I Can Just Be Me – Laura Story
5. Real Love – Blanca
6. I Receive – Israel Houghton
7. Moving Forward – Ricardo Sanchez
8. Breathe Your Name – Israel Houghton
9. Pressure – Jonathan McReynolds
10. Free to Be Me – Francesca Battistelli
11. Known – Tauren Wells
12. Lovin' Me – Jonathan McReynolds
13. Oceans (Where Feet May Fail) – Hillsong United
14. You Are Loved (Don't Give Up) – Josh Groban
15. Reckless Love – Cory Asbury

BONUS RESOURCE #2
Powerful Bible Verses on Your Identity in Christ

1. Psalm 3:3 – But thou, O LORD, art a shield for me; my glory, and the lifter up of mine head.

2. 1 Peter 5:6 – Humble yourselves therefore under the mighty hand of God, that he may exalt you in due time

3. Psalm 139:14 – I will praise thee; for I am fearfully *and* wonderfully made: marvellous *are* thy works; and *that* my soul knoweth right well

4. 1 Sam. 16:7 – But the LORD said unto Samuel, Look not on his countenance, or on the height of his stature; because I have refused him: for *the LORD seeth* not as man seeth; for man looketh on the outward appearance, but the LORD looketh on the heart

5. Jer. 29:11 – For I know the thoughts that I think toward you, saith the LORD, thoughts of peace, and not of evil, to give you an expected end

6. Genesis 1:27 – So God created man in his *own* image, in the image of God created he him; male and female created he them

7. Proverbs 4:23 – Keep thy heart with all diligence; for out of it *are* the issues of life

8. Ephesians 2:10 – For we are his workmanship, created in Christ Jesus unto good works, which God hath before ordained that we should walk in them

9. 1 Pet. 2:9 – But ye *are* a chosen generation, a royal priesthood, an holy nation, a peculiar people; that ye should shew forth the praises of him who hath called you out of darkness into his marvellous light

10. Heb. 10:35 – Cast not away therefore your confidence, which hath great recompence of reward

11. 2 Cor. 5:17 – Therefore if any man *be* in Christ, *he is* a new creature: old things are passed away; behold, all things are become new

12. Isaiah 62:3 – Thou shalt also be a crown of glory in the hand of the LORD, and a royal diadem in the hand of thy God

13. 1 Tim. 4:14 – Neglect not the gift that is in thee

14. 2 Tim. 1:7 – For God hath not given us the spirit of fear; but of power, and of love, and of a sound mind

15. Gen. 1:31 – And God saw everything that he had made, and, behold, *it was* very good

ABOUT THE AUTHOR

Known as The Dream Ambassador to many, Emem Washington's mission is to inspire, motivate, and cheer millions towards success, regardless of where they are, where they are from, or where they have been. She is a firm believer in the God who gave Joseph dreams of his own and made them come true.

In 2018, Emem co-authored the anthology *Women of Purpose*, a collection of inspiring stories to encourage readers to never give up on fulfilling their purpose in life. In addition to being an author, she is also a singer/songwriter, speaker, teacher, author, and attorney.

Having lived through and overcome several major difficult life situations, including two miscarriages and two stillbirths, fibroid surgery, being told she would no longer be able to conceive, a failed marriage, single motherhood, home fore-closure (to name a few personal trials), Emem uses the life lessons learned from those challenges to encourage and equip others to give up the stagnant, mediocre, suppressed life and to lead vibrant, truly alive lives. One of the ways that she does this is through speaking at events and also by and singing at events nationally and internationally.

She is happily married to Cedrick Washington and is the proud mom of two sons. When she is not teaching, researching, or leading worship, Emem enjoys spending time with her family, reading, and scribbling ideas on napkins and sticky notes. To get to know her more, visit her virtual home at www.ememwashington.com.